by

TROY AIKMAN

with Greg Brown

Illustrations by Doug Keith

SCHOLASTIC INC.

New York   Toronto   London   Auckland   Sydney

Greg Brown lives in Bothell, Washington, with his wife and two children. A sportswriter since 1979, Greg is the co-author of *Kirby Puckett: Be the Best You Can Be* and *Edgar Martinez: Patience Pays.*

Doug Keith has been an illustrator since 1982. His illustrations have appeared in national magazines, greeting cards, and books, and major sports teams have used his work in their promotions and advertising.

ISBN 0-590-67777-2

Text copyright © 1995 by Troy Aikman and Greg Brown.
Illustrations copyright © 1995 by Taylor Publishing.
All rights reserved. Published by Scholastic Inc., 555 Broadway, New York, NY 10012, by arrangement with Taylor Publishing Company.

12 11 10 9 8 7 6 5 4   6 7 8 9/9 0/0

Printed in the U.S.A.   08

First Scholastic printing, September 1995

Troy Aikman has donated all of his royalties from the sale of this book to the **Troy Aikman Foundation** *which benefits disadvantaged children.*

Helping kids...one dream at a time.

Troy at 8 years old

Computer imaging by Rob Hicks

My name is Troy Aikman, and I've written this book to share with you some of the lessons I've learned on my way to becoming the quarterback for the Dallas Cowboys football team.

I've endured many changes in my life.

My family moved from a city to a farm when I was 12, changing my dreams of becoming a professional baseball player.

I changed my focus to football and became the starting quarterback for two college football teams—the Oklahoma Sooners and the UCLA Bruins.

I was the No. 1 draft choice in the 1989 National Football League draft, but the Cowboys were 1–15 my first year.

I've had the worst rating of all NFL quarterbacks, and I've been the Most Valuable Player in the Super Bowl. I've been on the bottom and the top.

Through it all, I've learned everyone has to face the challenges of change. My hope is this book will help you face the changes in your life with a positive attitude.

was born Nov. 21, 1966, about two months before the first Super Bowl.

During my first year, my parents found it difficult to put on my shoes. They were not worried at first. Soon, however, they started to wonder why my legs slightly bowed below my knees and my toes curled under my feet.

They took me to Dr. Bill McColl, a former Chicago Bears football player, who told my parents I had a mild form of club foot.

Dr. McColl put casts on my feet when I was 8 months old. Every two weeks the casts were changed. I wore those casts until a month after my first birthday, and I even learned to walk wearing them.

After the casts came off, I wore special shoes until I turned 3 years old. The high-top white shoes looked like regular shoes except the toes pointed out, as though they were on the wrong feet. I wore the shoes day and night. My heels were strapped together when I slept.

Slowly my feet grew normally.

Despite my foot problems, I always had a ball in my hand. As far back as I can remember, I always loved sports and dreamed of being a professional athlete.

Aikman family photos

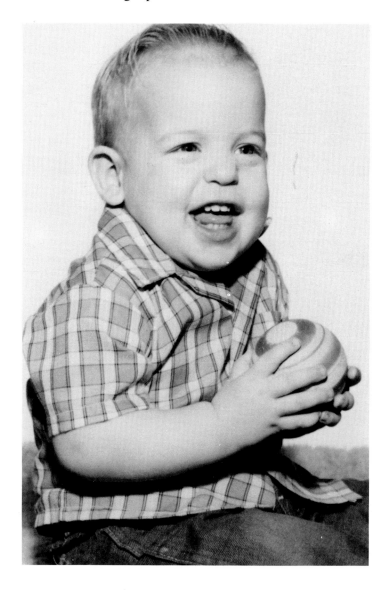

Where I grew up, in Cerritos, California, near Long Beach, we made our own fun. I did all the normal kid things, and, as you can see, I became a cowboy at an early age.

Dad worked long hours in pipeline construction, but on some weekends he took me hunting or fishing.

Most of all, I loved playing sports with my friends.

Play, play, play. That's all I wanted to do, though I was one of the youngest kids in the neighborhood.

You could say I was born to be an athlete.

I'd play hoops in our driveway with my two older sisters, Terri and Tammy, and friends. We'd ride bikes to a nearby park and play pickup baseball. We'd play touch football in front of our house for hours with the neighbor kids until we tired or someone scraped a knee. I just loved to play. Older kids played quarterback, and my oldest sister, Terri, could throw better than me.

You can see the chip in my early pictures. My sister Terri thinks I changed my smile to cover that tooth. Maybe subconsciously my tooth embarrassed me. Even today, I have a crooked smile, but so does my mom. Maybe I got it from her.

Aikman family

 The only time I got hurt badly in those days came in second grade. We were ready to play girls-against-boys in driveway basketball. A neighborhood bully yelled for the ball I was bouncing. I kept goofing around dribbling. He picked up a fist-sized rock and hurled it at me. I turned to him and the rock smashed into my mouth, cracking a front tooth in half.

ore than anything, I wanted to be a pro baseball player, as did all my friends. We all planned to play at the University of Southern California (USC) and then go to the major leagues. Three friends did make it to the major leagues.

Some days I would go to my room and practice signing my name. I wanted to be ready for the day someone asked for my autograph.

That might sound like a strange thing to do, but it helped me visualize my dream. I think it's important for everyone to have dreams and goals. If you dream, you might as well have big dreams.

At one of my first tee-ball games, my mom taught me the importance of having the right attitude to go with my dream.

During infield practice, a substitute coach made a change and brought a teammate from the outfield to play second base. I was at shortstop and yelled: "Don't put him there, he's no good."

My mom is one of the nicest people in the world. But she glared at me from where she sat in the bleachers after hearing what I said. You know the look parents give when they are upset. I had never seen her so angry.

I made a diving catch to save the game and everyone congratulated me afterward. Everyone except mom. She grabbed me by the back of the shirt, dragging me as we marched across the field to our car.

"If you ever do that again, I will pull you off the field and that will be the end of sports," she lectured, pounding the air with her finger on each word.

I learned behavior is one thing I could change. I never bad-mouthed another player.

The thought of not playing sports scared me, but death once frightened me more. When I was about 10, just after my grandfather died, I started to worry about dying. For about a month, thoughts of dying followed me like a shadow. I didn't tell anyone.

I know now it's best to talk to someone, anyone, when you feel that way.

Somehow I broke free from my worry. I'll bet there are things that frighten you. Everyone has fears.

Whatever troubles you, tell someone about it. It helps.

When I was younger, the freedom to sleep with my parents helped ease any nighttime fright.

I'd sometimes get up in the middle of the night and crawl into my parents' king-sized bed. I'd usually end up hogging the bed and covers.

My sisters would come in too when they were young, especially on Saturday mornings. That comforting warmth of family love always melted my fears and made me feel safe.

Soon I did not need that security of being close to my parents at night. I naturally grew out of the habit.

When I was 12, my sense of security about the future was yanked from me. My parents decided to move the family to Henryetta, Oklahoma.

Moving was upsetting to our whole family. If you have moved, you know how scary and difficult the change can be on everyone involved.

We left a sunny suburb of 50,000 people, where the beach, Knott's Berry Farm and playfields were a bike ride away. We landed in a town of 6,000 people on a 172-acre ranch with cows, pigs and chickens. Our new house was seven miles out of town on a dirt road.

Cristina Salvador

The Aikmans' house in California (far right).

The Aikmans' home in Oklahoma.

The change cost me my friends and my pro baseball dream, or so I thought.

I just knew my life was over. I resented my parents for moving. "How could they do this?" I thought.

Worse yet, we lived in a tiny trailer during the construction of our house.

I soon found out living on a ranch meant being responsible for chores. The one job I grew to hate was feeding the pigs.

Before school, I carried two buckets of slop to the pig pen. My arms tired every day.

That job lasted only a few months because we sold the pigs, but there were times I felt I'd be stuck feeding pigs the rest of my life.

Herman L. Brown

Aikman family

My attitude changed once I gave Henryetta a chance. I started eighth grade that fall and quickly felt right at home.

Small towns have a slower pace than cities. It gives people time to talk.

I found it easy to make new friends. I met Daren Lesley, and we became life-long buddies.

We became known as Ears and Foot. Long hair was the style, but I was one of the first in school to have my hair cut over my ears. Daren, well, he just had big feet.

I turned out for junior high football that first fall in Henryetta. It did not take long to realize that people in Oklahoma are crazy about football.

I had played quarterback since pee-wee football in California, but I was ready for a change. I decided not to tell the coaches about my quarterback experience. They put me at fullback.

The position change almost made me quit football. I was not experienced in blocking and being tackled. The fun of football was oozing out of me with each bruise.

One night I sat down and told Dad I was thinking about quitting football.

"Troy, I won't let you be a quitter," Dad said sternly. "If you don't want to play next year, fine, but once you start something you finish it. Finish the season."

I stuck with it and went back to the quarterback position the next season.

Aikman family

Herman L. Brown

I started my first varsity game as a 14-year-old sophomore for the Henryetta High School Fighting Hens.

I admit I was nervous. I learned quickly the best way to make those jittery feelings melt away is to concentrate on doing my job. When I focus on the task at hand, all the worry in my mind is forgotten.

I'll always remember winning that first game. It put me on top of the world.

I quickly came back down to reality.

Henryetta had a long tradition of losing football games. Opposing fans laughed at our Fighting Hens nickname and threw rubber chickens on the field. We continued losing that first year, winning only 4 and losing 6.

Troy led a come-from-behind victory in his first high school varsity game. Down by 4 points with just minutes to play, Troy threw a touchdown pass for the victory against Checotah.

My junior year we lost our first eight games, yet we still made the playoffs from our four-team division by winning our last two games.

It was the school's first playoff team in 25 years. "Two and eight and going to state" was our slogan. Although we lost in the first round, we changed tradition.

When I wasn't playing football, I loved watching the Dallas Cowboys play on TV. We lived about 200 miles north of Dallas, and the Cowboys were my team. One of my favorite players was quarterback Roger Staubach.

Even though I looked up to athletes, I believe the best role models are those people you can talk to every day, like your parents, a teacher or even a friend. My parents were my role models as I grew up.

After a tough one-point loss against Hartshorne, in which Troy threw a sidearm touchdown pass while being tackled, the opposing coach told him: "We'll be watching you someday on Monday Night Football."

We finished 6-4 my senior year. The city got all excited for us. Unfortunately, we missed the playoffs.

Fortunately, my passing did catch the eyes of college football coaches.

Oklahoma State coach Jimmy Johnson wanted me and almost talked me into being an OSU Cowboy. Instead, I decided to play for Barry Switzer at the University of Oklahoma. I believed the Sooners were ready to change their offense to add more passing to their traditional running offense.

After high school football seasons, I played center in basketball and shortstop or pitcher on the baseball team.

Football, however, became my favorite sport, and I set a goal to play in college.

After basketball games, even long road trips, I'd ask our coach for the gym keys. I'd lift weights late into the night to increase my strength for college football.

I focused on changing myself for the better. That kept me out of trouble.

While some classmates drank alcohol and tried drugs, I didn't. Illegal drugs change people for the worse, and that's one change I could live without.

My dad taught me many things, including how to weld. My first paycheck came from a welding job.

The best thing my parents taught me, however, wasn't a skill. They showed me how to have a positive attitude - to believe anything is possible.

Dad always said: "If you want something in life, if you're willing to pay the price, you can accomplish anything."

I have held onto that. I believed I could become a professional athlete, though I heard often how few people make it to the top.

My work habits came from living on our ranch. It taught me the value of work. Summers were my longest days. I'd haul hay from our fields during the day and play baseball at night. At times, I'd go back into the fields with Dad after a game until 2 o'clock in the morning.

Many Saturdays I worked at an auto shop in town to earn spending money.

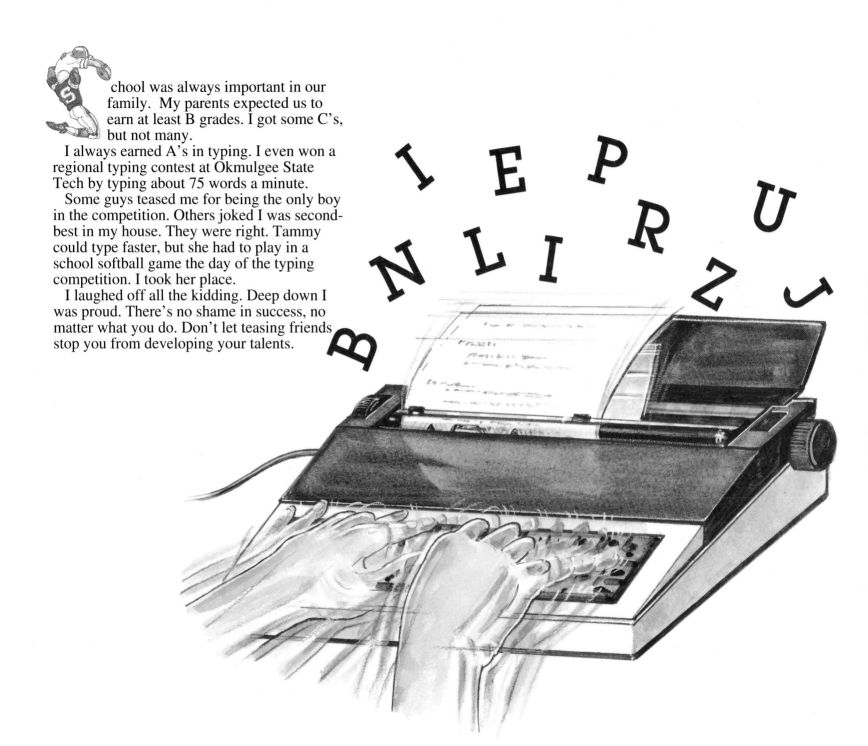

chool was always important in our family. My parents expected us to earn at least B grades. I got some C's, but not many.

I always earned A's in typing. I even won a regional typing contest at Okmulgee State Tech by typing about 75 words a minute.

Some guys teased me for being the only boy in the competition. Others joked I was second-best in my house. They were right. Tammy could type faster, but she had to play in a school softball game the day of the typing competition. I took her place.

I laughed off all the kidding. Deep down I was proud. There's no shame in success, no matter what you do. Don't let teasing friends stop you from developing your talents.

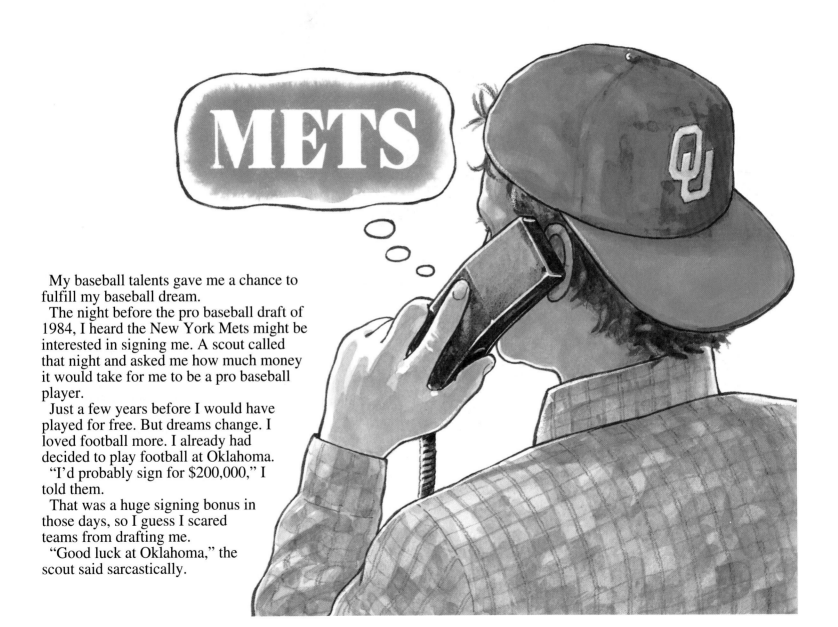

My baseball talents gave me a chance to fulfill my baseball dream.

The night before the pro baseball draft of 1984, I heard the New York Mets might be interested in signing me. A scout called that night and asked me how much money it would take for me to be a pro baseball player.

Just a few years before I would have played for free. But dreams change. I loved football more. I already had decided to play football at Oklahoma.

"I'd probably sign for $200,000," I told them.

That was a huge signing bonus in those days, so I guess I scared teams from drafting me.

"Good luck at Oklahoma," the scout said sarcastically.

Troy, 1984

University of Oklahoma

Not even luck would help me at Oklahoma. Unlike my high school start, my college debut was horrible. Injuries to quarterbacks ahead of me pushed me into the starting job for one game as a freshman before I was ready.

We played the University of Kansas Oct. 27, 1984. We were ranked No. 2 in the country, and I was the first freshman quarterback to start at Oklahoma in almost 40 years.

We lost 28-11. It was the Sooners' first loss on the Jayhawks' field in 20 years. I threw 14 passes, completing just two, for 8 yards. Kansas players picked off three passes, returning one for a touchdown.

Sooner fans grumbled. Many believed I did not have the right skills to lead Oklahoma. Some thought my career ended before it started.

The offseason lasted an eternity. I desperately wanted to prove what I could do.

In a strange way, that terrible game helped me grow up.

When things do not work out as planned, you can turn defeats into victories by using that pain as motivation to work harder.

Oklahoma entered the 1985 season rated No. 1 in the country. I earned the starting job and the pressure was on.

We won our first three games before facing Miami, coached by Jimmy Johnson, who had transferred from Oklahoma State.

I started hot, connecting on six of my first seven passes, one for a touchdown.

Moments later my season came to a painful end. Two Hurricanes tackled me, landing on my left leg

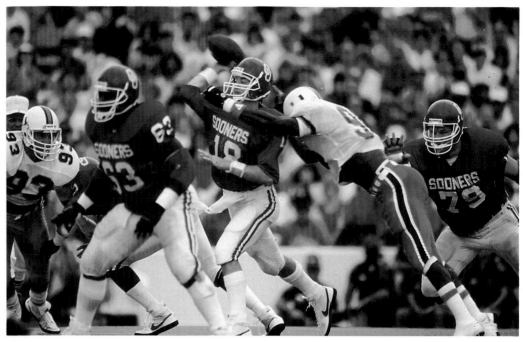

and breaking my ankle. We lost the game. Our speedy quarterback Jamelle Holieway stepped in and led the team to a national title.

I celebrated for my friends on the team, but it was difficult watching from the sidelines. The time off made me realize I had run into a dead end. Switzer had gone back to running the wishbone offense and Holieway would probably start the next season. It was time for a change.

I talked with coach Switzer and he agreed it would be best if I transferred to a school that passed more. Switzer called UCLA coach Terry Donahue and told him about me, which helped Switzer avoid a quarterback controversy.

Coach Johnson heard I might leave and asked me to come to Miami. I turned him down a second time. I was ready to go back to California.

Focus on Sports

I sat out one season at UCLA because of NCAA transfer rules. I practiced during the week, but on game day I watched from the stands. The only thing worse than losing is not playing. It was a rough year waiting my turn.

Unchanging love of God, family and friends helped me from being discouraged. My dad took a job in California the year before, so I spent some weekends with him and California relatives.

I called Daren, who was attending Northeastern State University in Oklahoma, a couple times a week.

My UCLA roommate, Doug Kline, and I became good friends. Doug, who played linebacker, came from Colorado. We both liked country music before country became cool. We took some heat for being two country boys in Los Angeles, but we figured we did not have to change who we were because of where we lived.

Aikman family

James D. Smith

That missed season I spent time working hard on becoming a better quarterback. It paid off the next two years. Once I got my chance to play, almost everything fell into place - except for two games.

Despite all the wins, we lost the two most important games. The goal every year for the UCLA football team is to play in the Rose Bowl, the granddaddy of all college bowl games.

Both years we were knocked out of the race for the roses by losses to cross-city rival USC.

Those losses were crushing. The first defeat happened on my 21st birthday - one of the worst days of my life. I played poorly in our 17-13 loss to the Trojans. I threw three interceptions all season until that game. USC picked off three passes that day.

That night, I flew home to Oklahoma. It was a tough period for me. I couldn't sleep for two weeks after the game. I replayed every mistake over and over in my head.

The setback could have destroyed my confidence, if I let it.

Bouncing back from those USC losses taught me one secret to success: History is one thing that never changes.

Learn from defeats, then shake them off like dust on cowboy boots. Once something happens, it's gone, and I move right along.

James D. Smith

James D. Smith

Troy and Emmitt Smith were named co-MVPs in the 1987 Aloha Bowl, and Troy was the MVP of the 1989 Cotton Bowl.

Playing in bowl games both years helped soothe those USC losses. The first was a 20-16 Aloha Bowl win in Hawaii against Florida. A Gator running back named Emmitt Smith had a big game against us, running for 128 yards.

The second introduced me to my future home. I played my last college game in Dallas at the Cotton Bowl, where we beat Arkansas 17-3. A few months later I returned to Dallas and signed an $11 million contract with the Dallas Cowboys. New owner Jerry Jones and new coach Jimmy Johnson, who I had rejected twice before, made me the No. 1 pick in the 1989 NFL draft. I felt humble and proud I made it to the NFL. I quickly set some new goals. The first was to help Dallas become winners again after three straight losing seasons.

Winning just one NFL game proved more difficult than I could imagine. I started the first four games, and we lost them all. In that fourth game, I broke my left index finger and missed six weeks.

In my first game back, I took one of the hardest hits I ever felt.

Blood dripped from my ear as I lay unconscious on the football field in 1989. I had just passed for an 80-yard go-ahead touchdown in what would have been my first NFL win. My moment of glory faded to black as a Phoenix Cardinal delivered a crushing blow. I was knocked out for 8 minutes. Phoenix won on a last-minute touchdown.

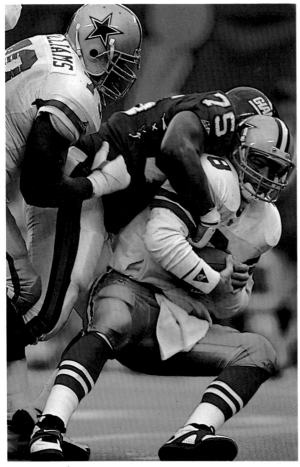

Focus on Sports

My head ached for days; my body and heart ached the whole season as everything went wrong. My rookie year we lost 15 of 16 games.

The one game we won, I was out with my broken finger. I took so many hits, I wondered how anyone could play in the NFL more than a few years.

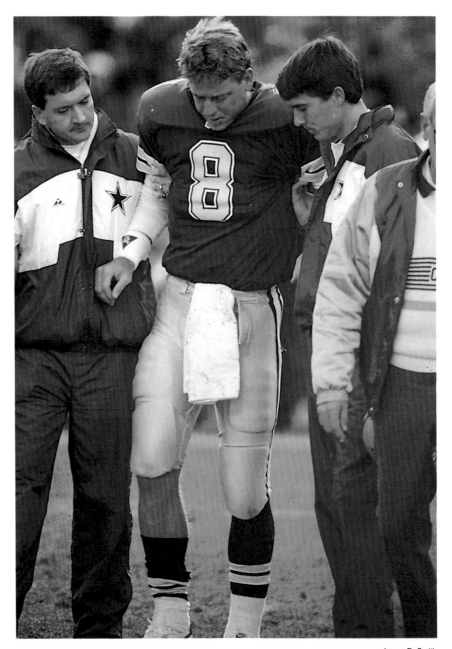

James D. Smith

8 TROY AIKMAN

AIKMAN

I'd faced rough years before, but this season was the worst. I dreamed so long and worked so hard to be a quarterback in the NFL, but nothing went right. My dream turned into a nightmare.

I finished my rookie season with the worst rating of all starting NFL quarterbacks.

Reading Terry Bradshaw's book about his days in the 1970s as quarterback of the Pittsburgh Steelers helped.

Knowing someone else had conquered the same problems I faced gave me encouragement not to give up.

During dark days, keep focused and have faith things will change.

The next season, the Cowboys drafted running back Emmitt Smith. His great running skill immediately gave our offense balance. We learned how to win and finished the 1990 season 7-9.

In 1991, Norv Turner became the new offensive coordinator. He brought a new system that we believed in and felt would utilize the talents of our team. The changes worked. We improved with an 11-5 season, losing to Detroit in the playoffs.

We started the 1992 season by beating defending Super Bowl champion Washington, and everything bounced our way for a change. We won 13 of 16 regular-season games and beat Philadelphia 34-10 in the first playoff contest.

We faced San Francisco in the National Football Conference championship, with the winner going to the Super Bowl. The 49ers had beaten us six straight times the past 12 years. That changed, too.

We won 30-20.

James D. Smith

James D. Smith

On the last day of the 1992 season, I was back on the same Rose Bowl field where I played for UCLA. The day was perfect, clear blue skies and warm sunshine, for Super Bowl XXVII.

I felt ready and relaxed until I walked through the tunnel and onto the field.

I have a quiet confidence during a contest, but before every game I do get that butterfly feeling in my stomach.

On Super Bowl Sunday, it felt like a flock of birds in my gut.

Everything was a blur at the start. I felt the gaze of millions watching on TV and the 98,374 screaming fans at the game. I almost passed out in the first quarter because I was breathing so hard.

Somehow I got through it by keeping my focus on what I needed to do moment by moment.

Rick Stewart All-Sport USA

AP/Wide World Photo

AP/Wide World Photo

The thought of losing entered my mind early in the game when the Bills went ahead 7-0. My passing was off as I completed just three of my first six. I felt uncomfortable.

During a break, I talked with Coach Turner. He said we needed to change our passing plans. The Bills were taking away the outside passes, so we threw more to the middle.

We started moving the ball, and our team got into our rhythm.

We scored on a touchdown pass in the first quarter to tie it 7-7. From there everything went our way.

Our defense was outstanding, scoring two touchdowns on recovered fumbles.

Our 52-17 victory ranks as one of the most lopsided in Super Bowl history.

Winning Super Bowl XXVII was a tremendous natural high that lasted the whole offseason. Being on top did not last long enough.

    I hurt my back lifting weights in the offseason and needed back surgery, which was successful. I pushed myself to be ready when the season started. Emmitt Smith, however, missed the first two games settling his contract. We lost both games.

  No team had won a Super Bowl after an 0-2 start. We changed that. With the return of Emmitt, we rolled to the playoffs.

Again, we faced the 49ers in the NFC title game. And again we won, this time 38-21.

Strangely, I don't remember anything about the game. That's because the knee of 300-pound 49er Dennis Brown smacked into the side of my helmet, knocking me out of the game early in the third quarter. I remained awake in a haze of confusion on the sidelines and had trouble remembering things.

I spent the night at Baylor University Medical Center. Someone asked if I knew the site of the upcoming Super Bowl. I said, "Henryetta?"

When that made the news, people in Henryetta had some fun with it. They sold tickets for a pretend Super Bowl in Henryetta to raise money for youth projects.

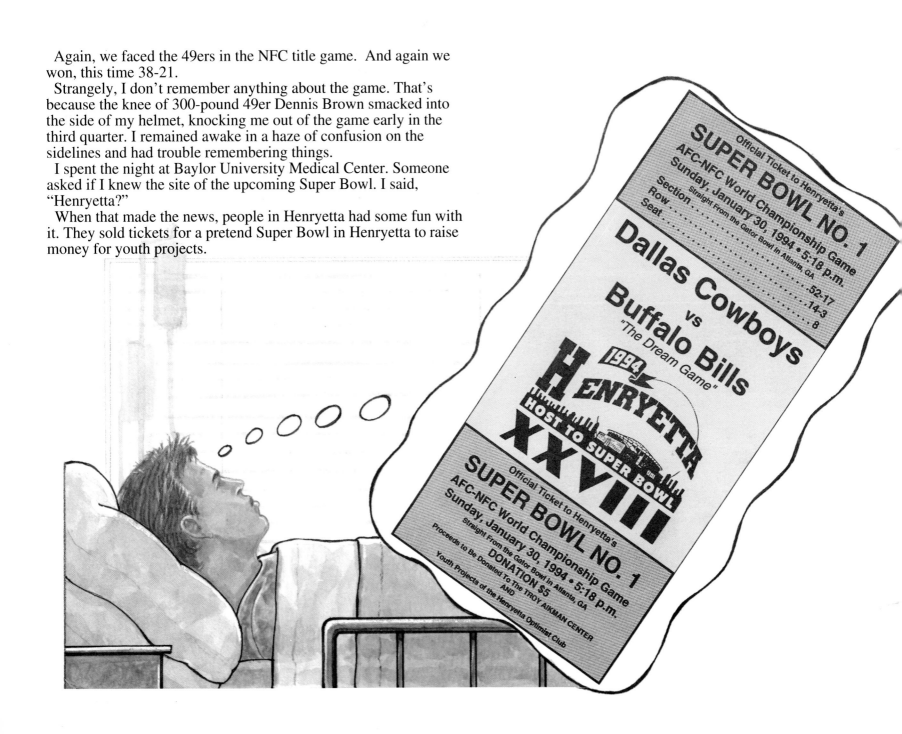

The next day I felt better and traveled to Atlanta with the team to prepare for Super Bowl XXVIII and a rematch against Buffalo.

I did not feel 100 percent during practices. There are many times in football and life when you have to function even when you are hurting. For me, this was one of those times.

Some people think playing in pain makes me tough. Maybe I'm just hard-headed.

Whatever toughness I have comes from my dad. He is the toughest guy I know. He never missed a day of work.

James D. Smith

The first two quarters it looked as though maybe I should have taken the day off. My timing was rusty and we were frustrated, down 13–6 at halftime.

The game turned on a fumble return for a touchdown by James Washington in the third quarter. Emmitt picked up his pace in the second half and earned the MVP award as we won 30-13.

Two Super Bowls, two victories. That's almost too much to believe after winning just one game four years before.

Troy completed 19 of 27 passes for 207 yards in Super Bowl XXVIII. His two-year post-season performances set three NFL records: highest rating (111.2), completion percentage (71.1%) and yards per attempt (8.53).

Focus on Sports

The Dallas Morning News/John Rhodes

The 1994 season blindsided us with change. Coach Jimmy Johnson left the team in the offseason, replaced by my former Oklahoma coach, Barry Switzer. Norv Turner became the new coach for Washington. Several key players became free agents and went to other teams.

A rash of injuries hampered several starters during the season, and I missed two weeks with a knee injury.

On top of everything, we dealt with the pressure to be perfect, which no one can fulfill.

Despite all the adversity, we won our division with a 12–4 record, the same as the season before. The first three losses might have been wins if three plays had gone our way—a referee's call, one pass and one extra inch.

The media and some fans doubted us at playoff time. One magazine proclaimed: "Dallas is Dead."

We showed everyone we had some life left by beating Green Bay 35–9.

That set up a third straight showdown against San Francisco with the Super Bowl at stake.

No team in NFL history had won three straight Super Bowls. There was no doubt in my mind the Cowboys could rewrite history.

But the 49ers were strong. They cruised through the season with a league-best 13-3 record. Plus they beat us during the season to earn home-field advantage for our NFC title game.

All-Sport

James D. Smith

Before I even dirtied my uniform on the soggy San Francisco grass, I looked up at the scoreboard and we were behind 21–0.

The 49ers picked off my third pass for a touchdown and two quick fumbles led to two more 49ers touchdowns in the game's first 7½ minutes.

"Hey, we're fine," I told teammates on the sidelines. "We're going to win this thing. We're not out of it."

We fought back with everything we had. Three times we cut the lead to 10 points and outscored the 49ers 14–7 in the second half. But every time we'd get close, they'd block our momentum.

With 1 minute, 56 seconds to play, we still had a chance. We moved the ball to the 49er 46 and faced fourth down and 18 yards to go. Until that last pass, I believed we would win.

But we fell short. We lost 38-28.

Troy earned his fourth Pro Bowl invitation in 1994. His 94-yard TD pass against Green Bay was the longest in playoff history. His 53 passes and 380 yards against S.F. set team playoff records and were career bests.

After the game, I met 49er quarterback Steve Young on the field and said: "I'm happy for you. Good luck against San Diego." Fate had given Steve his chance at Super Bowl history.

Losing such a big game is painful and leaves an empty feeling. It hurts worse when a team makes mistakes as we did.

Still, I felt proud to be a Cowboy that day. I walked tall off the field. We had given our best and never quit, just as we had done all season.

Some say our 1994 season was not a success. I never will. I'm more proud of the '94 team than our Super Bowl teams. We were champions over change.

You can be a champion, too. As you run with your talent, run hard, run with courage and run as far as you can, then you will be a champion in your heart. Even when things change.